I Am Big

by Jay Dale
illustrated by Amanda Gulliver

"I am big," said Lea.
"I can go on this slide."

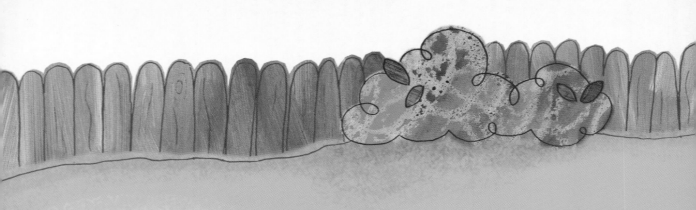

3

"I am big," said Lea.
"I can go on this swing."

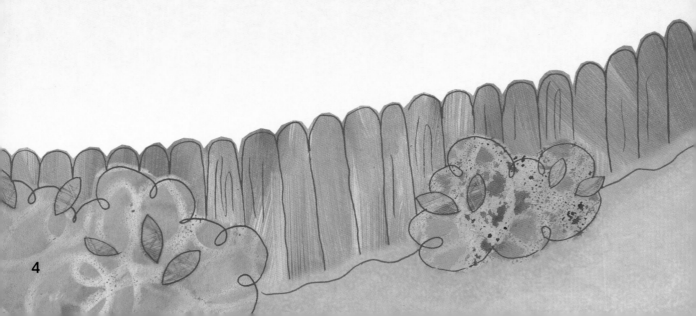

"I am big," said Lea.
"I can go on this boat."

"I am big," said Lea.
"I can go on this ladder."

"I am big," said Lea.
"I can go on this bridge."

"I am big," said Lea.
"I can go on this train."

"I am big," said Lea.
"I can play
in the playhouse."